Entrepreneurship

The Definitive Beginner's Bundle

How To Become An Entrepreneur And Master The Fundamentals With These Essential Guides

By Adam Richards

ISBN-13: 978-1533495907
ISBN-10: 1533495904

Table of Contents

Small Business

The Rookie Entrepreneur's Guide

How To Start Your Own Business 10 Step Action Plan

By Adam Richards

Introduction

So, you've finally decided to take the plunge and venture into the entrepreneurial boots that have been waiting for you all this while. There's a thing or two that you need to know about the terrain that you will soon be in the process of navigating; it's really a lot rougher than you think it is and if you're not careful, you might just end up wishing that you had never made that foray into the business world, after all.

This book is an attempt to help you ensure that the business you do finally start will be a profit-making machine, much like you always dreamed it would be. It will help you ensure that you take just the right 'steps' towards tailoring that business of yours for success, overcoming all the tiny obstacles that come in your way, that cumulatively have a rather gargantuan effect in restraining you to reach your full business potential. Think of it as a guide towards creating the lucrative small business, you always dreamed of.

In the end it is experience that we all must make a point of learning from; the great part about having this invaluable book is that you get all the experience you need without even having to make the mistakes that you would otherwise have to make in the process of garnering that high level of experience. You will learn how to do the 'right' things and not the wrong ones when it comes to the process of planning and setting up that business of yours, ensuring that you are well on the path to unbridled success in the realm of your small business.

Let's begin, then, and 'climb that staircase' step by step, towards entrepreneurial success!

Chapter 1:

Step One – Idea Generation

One might think that it would be absolutely essential to have a great idea as far as it comes to setting up a business that will reap great dividends over time, right? Well, you couldn't be further from the truth if you thought the same. In fact, some of the best ideas are really the most common ones – the tried and tested, the ones that actually work.

All you need to do is take a great idea that is already existing out there, and then put an entirely new spin on it so that you pack a punch where it comes to achieving success in your work out there. In fact, by doing so you are really creating your own unique business idea. Let's take a look, then, at the process of idea generation and all that it entails in order to make it successful!

Personal Evaluation

This is extremely important when it comes to the successful idea generation for your business. At first you must take out the desired amount of time to actually spend on brainstorming what you are truly passionate about. Once you have found out the same, you have to see if your skill sets matches up to the 'idea' that you have thought of; it might not be a very good idea to pursue something that you might not be best equipped to do.

Once you have aligned your skill sets with the idea that you imagine could catapult you to entrepreneurial fame, you have to see if there is a real 'need' out there for the product or service that you are proffering to offer. If there is, you know that you are headed in the right direction!

Assessment from external sources

You might wish to look up to people like peers and your family in order to get the best possible advice as to whether the business idea you have chosen in the point above, is really indeed most worthy of the merit that you have bestowed upon it, or not.

You have to understand that by doing this you get an unbiased 'outside perspective' on your proposed business idea in the form of things like constructive criticism that might go a long way in ensuring that your idea does indeed hold water and that you are well poised towards launching your new venture. You might wish to talk to a few entrepreneurs as well; they have been there and done that and they will most certainly be able to offer you the best possible advice on how to take that idea of yours forward in the smoothest manner possible.

Consider all possibilities

The very fact that you have a brilliant idea does in no way imply that you are 'sorted' when it comes to being on the path to entrepreneurial success. You have to understand that there will be a lot of hurdles along the way, which could indeed lead to a lot of disappointment should things go askew in the process of setting up that business. Of course you need to be mentally prepared for the same; the last thing you want is to be discouraged by the potential hurdles that come along your path, to the point where you want to throw it all away.

By being apprised of the hurdles that might come along, you are preparing yourself to be a lot more resilient than you otherwise would have been, thus paving the way for you to face any obstacle that might come your way. In fact, some of the most successful entrepreneurs out there are those that have embraced failure time and again, simply because they believed to the core in the ideas that they felt would change the world.

Of course it is vital that you have a great business idea to begin with. Sometimes you might just get that 'Eureka!' moment when you're sitting in a mall and observing things around you. But in addition to the pointers that we have discussed, one also needs to do a thorough amount of research into the idea that they have stumbled upon, in order to assess its viability in the market out there. The following chapter is an endeavor in just that. Let's take a look!

Chapter 2: Step Two – Proper And Solid Research

Of course you must do an adequate amount of research into that small business idea of yours that you believe is going to reap 'big' dividends for you. Not doing so would only be akin to walking in the dark. Let's take a look, then, at how we can do the requisite amount of research that is required to literally 'confirm' that business idea of ours while at the same time lighting the path that will take it to fruition.

Research that 'industry'

Make sure that you 'research' your industry well. Of course the goal would be to 'research here', but it must be specific towards the industry that your business idea is associated with. You have to understand if the market that you are entering is growing or declining, and what are all the latest trends in the same industry. That will give you an idea of where you are really poised, as far as the industry you are planning to enter is concerned.

Research your 'target customers'

You might be catering to a particular niche and by researching your target audience based on factors like income levels and demographic factors, you will be able to get a solid idea of just how 'big' your target audience really is. The same goes if you are in the process of selling your goods online to a national or international audience; you have to understand the kind of numbers you are catering to out there.

Research your 'competition'

This is one of the most important things you could do. Make sure that you create a SWOT analysis so that you will be able to understand your competitors' strengths and weaknesses and how they might present opportunities and/or threats to your business. You might wish to keep an eye on that indirect competition out there, as well. For instance, if you're opening a fast food restaurant in a mall then you might wish to keep an eye on the fine dining restaurants in the mall as well, who might eat into that slice of 'pie' that you wish to carve out of the whole, for your very own.

Make sure you do those 'surveys'

Conducting surveys is one of the best possible methods that you could employ to understand what your potential customers out there really want; make sure that you use those online survey tools like SurveyMonkey and PollDaddy in order to get the best possible results. You could poll your customers on your website or even via email. The results that you accrue in this process will most certainly be most invaluable to you when it comes to getting valuable data for your business needs.

Have those 'focus groups'

Having a focus group is pretty much like doing a survey, but it is with a limited number of participants (usually not more than 10) and is far more in depth. You can ask those people in the focus group as to what they think about things like price points, advertising campaigns and service features. Of course you can have the meeting for up to 90 minutes, which helps you get more than the data you possibly need in order to understand that potential customer of yours. Of course you will have to pay them for their time, but you will see in time that it is well worth it!

Get help

Sometimes you will find that you might really get the best possible help from local colleges and universities. All you have to do is approach them for help and you might find that they are more than eager to do that market research for you as part of their research for a class project. You will be guaranteed a most high level of market research if they do.

Of course it is most important that a good deal of research be done before we even think of venturing out there in the business arena. It helps give you that much needed sense of clarity to move forward in the right direction and meet your business goals and objectives!

Chapter 3: Step Three – The Business Plan

Now that you've done all the relevant market research that is needed to meet those business objectives of yours, the time has come to effectively plan your foray into the business arena so that you go through every step of the process in the best possible manner and with the least possible glitches.

Let's take a look at how we can effectively 'plan' our small business in order to take it forward.

In essence, this means that we have to create a business plan in order to ensure that we are highly consolidated in our approach to taking things forward and most prepared for any eventuality that might befall us during the course of taking that business of ours forward. Let's look at the things we need to keep in consideration when preparing the same.

You Must have a concise plan

Make sure that the plan is as concise as can possibly be, while at the same time ensuring that you do not miss any of the important details. If you're going to be showing that plan of yours to an investor, you really do need to trim all that fluff because it will only deter them from the process of reading it. So keep it to the point and simple.

Make sure that all the key areas are covered

You want to ensure that you do not miss any area that needs to be covered in that business plan of yours. Thus the areas like Company, Product/Service, Market, Competition, Management Team, Marketing, Operations and Financials should be covered in detail. Make sure that you use color charts and spreadsheets in order to make the relevant information presented in each of the sections far easier to understand.

Pay attention to the USP of your business

You have to convince the investor out there why it is indeed worth his or her salt to invest their money in that project of yours by showing them the USP (Unique Selling Proposition) of your product that will enable them to see just why that product or service of yours is worth investing in, as opposed to them merely keeping their money in a bank or investing in something like shares, in order for the same to grow.

Pay attention to those sales projections

While you will find that the costs are really rather easy to document, it is the sales projections that really need to be as conservative and realistic as possible. Make sure that you make a simple cash-flow and break even chart that will help you and anyone else who reads it gain a simple understanding into how many sales you need in order to cover your costs, and how much financing you need to raise in order to start up successfully.

The thing to remember here is that a lot of sales are on credit cards and that it might take up to four weeks to realize the cash thus collected; make sure you make those financial projections in tune with the same.

Executive Summary

Often this is presented at the beginning of the business plan and it is highly recommended that you do the same; but it is highly recommended that you begin the business plan with that executive summary because this is the thing that most investors will look to first, in an attempt to determine if they want to read further. They are strapped of time and so you need to make sure that this 'pitch' of yours strikes a solid punch and makes them thirsty for more. The executive summary in essence is nothing but a summary of that entire business plan of yours. It's like the plan in a nutshell.

Finally it must be emphasized that you really do need to stick to that business plan of yours, if you need to ensure that you are on the right path to success. That is because you have most clearly defined your business goals and objectives in it and thus it needs to be continually reviewed in order to ensure that you are indeed on the right track as far as it comes to implementing those goals and objectives.

Chapter 4: Step Four – Getting Your Finances In Order

Now that you have your business plan ready, it's time to take things forward and set the ball rolling. Oh, did anyone mention that there might be money involved?

Of course, there will be!

Here's a look at the tips to ensure that your finances are up to the mark when it comes to funding your business endeavor.

Make sure that you budget your spending

You need to know how much money you need in order to break even and how much you need to spend in order to run your business on a daily basis. That budget of yours needs to be divided into four key areas: prospective income, fixed expenses, variable expenses and pay cheque-allowance. Make sure that you do not go overboard by having a good sense of balance between what you need and what you want.

Make sure that you invest well

You need to make sure that you invest that hard-earned money of yours on things that have long-term advantages. But of course you need to make sure that you balance well the cost against the return on the investment.

If the investment does not give you a significant return in terms of improving the quality of your business, then it might very well be worth revising your decision to make the same.

It is always better to 'invest' as opposed to 'spending' on things that will only give you benefits in the short term.

Make sure that you maintain those records well

A lot of times people find themselves at a loss to procure receipts of old simply because they did not take the effort to keep them in the first place. Make sure that you file away each and every receipt that might turn out to be helpful for you in the time to come.

You can also use an app that lets you upload your receipts and get access to an image of the receipt that you want whenever you want it, in that accounting system of yours.

Make sure that your personal and business bank accounts are kept separate

You will find that if you don't, it is easy to lose track of where that cash is coming from and you will find out much later on that you have been funding your business for some time through your own personal reserves. You might wish to avoid something like this happening by paying your business expenses with a dedicated business credit card with a fixed credit limit. This will give you the control to plan those cash in-flows of your business in order to meet those cash out-flows.

Cut down on those 'fixed' costs

It's really those 'fixed costs' that need to be worked on in an attempt to trim them, in order to ensure that that profitability of yours is not being eaten into. Thus you might wish to use 'Skype' instead of travelling long distances for those business meetings, whenever it is possible to do so. Or you might choose to use equipment that 'does the job' rather than procure fancy equipment that has way more features than you need and looks aesthetically more appealing. That way, you can make sure you cut down on unnecessary costs while at the same time ensuring there is no compromise at all in terms of the quality that is afforded to the customer out there.

Make sure that you create the right legal structure

When you're in the process of starting that small business of yours, you want in all probability to start out as a 'sole proprietor', because it really doesn't cost any money, as you don't have to pay to create corporate documents and tax returns. Of course, over the course of time you might have to change the structure of your business, depending on how it grows.

Make sure you get insurance if you need it

If you're operating out of your home, you won't really need it, but if you are operating from an office outside home, then you will need that minimum insurance on your office and assets.

Chapter 5: Step Five – Choosing A Business Structure

In the previous chapter, we touched upon how we should create the right legal structure in order to ensure our finances are well taken care of; in this chapter, we will further explore this point in an attempt to understand exactly what kind of structure we need to assign to that fledgling business of ours, so that it can be primed in the best possible manner for success in the time to come. Let us take a look at the different types of business structures out there, with a view to understanding which one will work out best for us.

Types of Business Structures

A sole proprietorship, as earlier discussed, offers complete managerial control to the owner.

A partnership is a business structure that involves two or more people that agree to share in the profits and losses in a business.

A corporation is a legal entity that is created to conduct business. The corporation is an entity that is separate from the people that founded it.

LLC (Limited Liability Company) is a hybrid form of business structure that is increasingly gaining popularity. It allows the owners to take advantages of the perks afforded by both the partnership and corporation types of business structures.

Choosing a Business Structure

When it comes to the process of choosing a business structure from the ones that are outlined above, the following considerations need to be kept in mind.

Risks and Liabilities

In the case of your business providing services that are particularly risky, such as the trading of stocks, it would be most prudent to go in for an LLC, which will serve to protect your assets from business debts and claim. You might wish to go in for a 'corporation' type of structure, as well.

Formalities and Expenses

If you're starting a company on a shoestring budget, it is highly recommended that you go in for a sole proprietorship or a partnership. You do not wish to go in for an LLC here because it will be far more expensive to create and more difficult to maintain, as well. In the case of sole proprietorships and partnerships, however, you don't really have to fill in any forms or pay any fees in order to start your business. Also, there are no special operating rules out there that you are needed to follow.

Income Taxes

In the case of paying taxes, you will find that sole proprietorships, partnerships and LLCs all pay their taxes on business profits in the same way. All the profits and losses encountered herein pass from the business to the owners, who report their share of the profits on their personal income tax returns. The owners of these businesses must pay taxes on all the net profits of the business, irrespective of the amount of money they take out of the business each year.

However, the owners of a corporation pay taxes only on the profits they actually receive, such as in the case of bonuses, dividends and salaries. The corporation itself pays taxes at special corporate rates on the profits that are left in the company. And owing to the fact that corporations enjoy a lower tax rate than most individuals for the first $50000 to $75000 of corporate income, a corporation and its members might have a lower tax bill than that of the owners of an unincorporated business that earns the same level of profit.

Investment needs

Only a corporation will allow you to sell ownership shares in the company through those ‘stock options’ that makes it easier to procure investment and also retain employees within the organization. But if you are not envisaging your company to ever go public, you don’t have to consider this option at all.

Of course there is no reason to believe that once you create the structure for your organization, it cannot be changed. You might start out small as a sole proprietorship or partnership and then as your business grows and your risk of liability increases, you might wish to convert it to an LLC or a corporation.

Chapter 6: Step Six - Selecting And Registering Your Business Name

Now that you've chosen the appropriate business structure for the organization that you have proposed, you need to give it life by christening it with a name, right? Of course once that is done it will have to be registered as well, and then you will finally have the sense of your company being 'born', in the process. Let's take a look at all the steps that will be required to get us through the process.

Naming your small business

Of course the very first step would be to come up with a credible name for your business. You need to understand that having the right name is really most essential when it comes to your business; it might just provide that edge that you need over the competition, after all. Let's take a look on how we can effectively come up with a stellar business name.

Use a name that conveys a benefit

In case you are selling a product out there that you feel has a real tangible benefit that is its USP, you might wish to incorporate it as part of that product name, in order for it to have the desired effect on your target audience. In case you are opening an 'exotic' organic store, for example, you might wish to include the word 'exotic' as part of that name, for instance, so that you convey that which you are trying to sell out there in the most succinct fashion.

Use 'words' and not 'initials'

Unless you're a hugely successful corporation like IBM, initials won't do much towards portraying a rather stellar image of your brand out there. Make sure that you steer clear of them.

Make sure that it can be trademarked

You might wish to check up USTPO.gov before settling on the name that you have in mind. In case you are looking to make your brand big, you really need to make sure that the name can be trademarked.

Test it on Google AdWords

When you test the name you have shortlisted on Google AdWords, you get a list of similar search phrases along with how many global and monthly searches each is getting. This will also help to ensure that there is not a slightly similar word that will get far more attention than yours on the Internet.

Registering your Small Business Name

Now that you have gotten hold of an appropriate name for your small business, the time has come to register it so that you can finally move ahead with your business plans. In the case of having a sole proprietorship, you will find that it is not required to register your business name at the state level.

However, many states require that sole proprietors use their own name for the business until they formally file another name. This is known as your DBA (Doing

Business As). However, in the case of a corporation, limited liability company or even partnership you will find that you will have to register your business name with the State. This will ensure that no other corporation, limited liability company or partnership out there will be able to use the name that you have chosen.

Now that your official business name has been registered, if you want to sell products or services under a different name, then you have to file an assumed name certificate or a fictitious name statement. This is also needed if you want to use your LLC name without the suffix 'Limited Liability Company' or 'LLC'. In most states an LLC will file its fictitious name statement with the Secretary of State or Department of Corporations.

However, in some states the LLC needs to file a 'Doing Business As' certificate with the city clerk. In order to see where your LLC must file an assumed name certificate in your state, you have to go to the website of the 'U.S. Small Business Administration'.

Registering your business name as a trademark will ensure that no other business out there can take your name or one that's glaringly similar and you can do this with the U.S. Patent and Trademark Office.

Chapter 7: Step Seven – Necessary Licenses And Permits

Okay, so now you've gotten a name for that business of yours and even gone ahead and registered it out there in an attempt to get started as soon as you possibly can. So now what? Before you begin, there are certain things that you need to bear in mind, such as procuring the all important permits and licenses that are needed in order to make sure nothing gets in the way of your business when it is up and running. Let's take a look at all the licenses and permits that are required when it comes to running that small business of ours.

Business License

You need to contact your city's business license department and pay them a fee to procure that business license which grants you the permission to operate that business of yours in the city. What happens when you file that application for the license is, the city planning or zoning department will check to make sure that your area is zoned for the purpose that you wish to use it for and that there are enough parking spaces that are required to meet the codes.

In case an area is not zoned for your proposed business, then you will need to get a variance or a conditional-use permit. For that you will have to present your case before the city planning commission. As long as you show that your business will in no way disrupt the sanctity of the neighborhood where you propose to set up shop, it will be pretty easy to get that permit.

Fire Department Permit

You will have to get this one if your business involves the use of any flammable materials or if it will be open to the public. You will find that in some cities you have to get this permit even before you start your business; in others, all you have to do is schedule periodic inspections of your premises to ensure that they do indeed meet fire safety regulations.

Businesses that do the same include restaurants and day-care centers, places where a lot of people usually tend to congregate.

Air And Water Pollution Control Permit

In case your business involves the burning of materials, disposal of waste into sewers and even possibly involve the use of products that produce gas, you will need this permit.

Sign Permit

In some cities there are certain sign ordinances that restrict the size, location and even the type of lighting and sign that you might be using outside your business premises. You might wish to check with your landlord and get his or her written approval before you even think of putting that sign out there.

County Permits

If your business is located outside a city or town, these permits will be applicable to you. The county governments usually require the same kinds of licenses and permits that businesses need in cities, but at the same time the regulations in counties are not all that strict as those in cities.

State Licenses

In many states, you will find that people in certain occupations will be needed to have specific licenses or occupational permits. They might even have to pass state examinations before they can procure these licenses and start operating their businesses. These are generally applicable to people who provide personal services, such as insurance agents, barbers and cosmetologists.

Federal Licenses

There are a few businesses out there that require federal licenses, such as meat processors and radio and TV stations. The Federal Trade Commission will tell you if your business needs the same.

Sales Tax License

You need this 'certificate of resale' because any home-based business selling goods must pay taxes on the goods thus sold. In some states it's a criminal offense to operate without one, so make sure you get this before you open the doors to your business.

Health Department Permit

If you are in the business of supplying food to people either through a restaurant or through a wholesale business, you need this one. It costs around $25 and varies depending on the size of your business and the amount and size of the equipment you possess.

Chapter 8: Step Eight - Location, Location, Location

Of course you've gotten a gist of all the licenses and permits that you will be needing when it comes to setting up your small business; what you need to bear in mind, though, is the fact that you might want to hold onto actually 'procuring' those licenses until you have found the absolute best location for your business.

The location of your business is integral in ensuring its success; you don't want to make a mistake by rushing in too soon and getting it wrong. Let's look at the ways in which we can ensure that we hit just the right 'spot' where it comes to finding that stellar location for our business.

Choose the most 'conducive' location

You have to do the obvious where it comes to choosing the right location, and that entails choosing one where there is increased consumer traffic in the case of the 'retailer' and one where there is easy access to suppliers and transport routes for the manufacturer. You cannot miss the obvious when it comes to securing the right location – make sure that you select a most conducive area to set up shop!

Make sure that it is 'financially' viable

No matter how great a location you might have zoned in on in an attempt to get the perfect spot for your business, it might not really be all that financially viable.

Remember, one must always keep their financial considerations first; you can settle for a less attractive area and keep that outstanding area that you have shortlisted for future reference.

Also, the property value is not the only thing that you need to bear in mind when securing your location; you have to be aware of the taxes as well. It might be significantly cheaper to operate in another city with more lenient taxation laws.

Of course the 'move' to another city might also mean that you have to charge less for your goods, so make sure you make this decision after giving it a good deal of thought.

Rent 'smart'

In the case of most businesses that are operating for the very first time in the field of retail, it might make a lot of sense to rent a space in a mall where you are ensured of a large number of footfalls. But you need to be warned – the rents might be so large that they can 'kill', and it might really be in your best interest to rent space in a mall that is not all that high end in the beginning, so that you don't pay all that much on rent.

Security

You have to ensure that the place you have selected is most 'safe'. The last thing you want is to put off customers by locating your business in a place where they are scared to venture into.

You need to make sure that you select a place that has a high level of security; one that will make both your team members and clients feel at ease.

Make sure that you inspect that property you have selected

You need to actually go out there and inspect the property that you have shortlisted, before you venture into a deal to secure the same. You have to see if looks as good in reality as it does on paper. Sometimes what you see and what you get can be two completely different things.

Play smart by locating next to the competition

Really? You might be thinking. Yes, that's just about the smartest move you could ever make. If you are in a business that deals in a specific industry such as travel, you might wish to locate in an area that is the proverbial 'Mecca' of the travel industry. That way half your work is already done; you will see that you get a lot more customers in the process than you would if you were located far away.

Think 'convenience'

If you are a family person then you would like your workplace close to home; if you are going to be using public transport you want a central location!

Chapter 9: Step Nine - Choosing An Accounting System

Now that you're secure in the location your business needs to be in, you might want to take a look 'within' and scrutinize that business itself; it often involves a lot of mundane clerical work that is most efficiently managed by some top notch accounting software that you can choose to meet your accounting needs.

You will find that you will save a lot of time and have far more accurate records, if you use that accounting software as opposed to doing things manually.

Let's take a look, then, at the things we need to bear in mind when choosing that accounting system.

Narrow down those software choices

You can do this by taking stock of the services that are offered by the accounting systems out there, and choosing one that is best suited to your needs.

You will find that most of the accounting systems cover the following features.

Inventory management

Sales tracking

Managing customer contacts

Merchant account support to accept credit card payments

Budgeting

Estimates

Payroll

Business tax reporting

Industry-specific accounting systems

You have to keep in mind that there are certain accounting systems out there that are especially tailored for the kind of industry that you find yourself in. It might be a smart move to go in for one of these.

Thus if you find yourself in diverse fields like manufacturing and wholesale, you will find that there are software packages that are customized to cater to each one of these in a way that the individual requirements are met in specific and not covered in general like through certain accounting systems out there.

Talk to others

You will find other people in the same industry as yours using accounting software; make sure that you talk to them about the perks and disadvantages of the accounting software they use. That will help you make a choice far easier when it comes to zoning down on the best accounting software for your needs.

At the same time you will come to realize that there is really no software that is perfect; there are simply those that are better suited to your needs than others. Make sure that you talk to as many people as you possibly can about their accounting systems before you come your decision.

Find out whether it will grow with your business

You need to know if the software that you are looking at has modules that can be incorporated into it at a later stage; a common module that is incorporated in later stages is that of 'payroll accounting'.

In case the module cannot be added, you want to ensure that the accounting software is capable of being upgraded to a more efficient version, easily.

It should be compatible with your bank

You want to ensure that the accounting software that you have chosen works with your bank, because of the ease with which transactions can be downloaded from your bank, saving you a lot of time in the process.

Choosing between online and desk accounting software

Online software is the kind of accounting software that runs securely through a web browser. It is especially suited to those who are accessing accounting data and records from multiple computers, as opposed to the other 'desk accounting' type of software.

Can that access be restricted?

You might want one person to have absolute control over that accounting software in the sense that he or she can access all its areas; however, you might wish to afford some level of control to others in the organization to things like data entry.

At the same time you might not want them to have access to those 'reports' and you need to make sure that there is a system in place whereby you can give them 'selective access' to the software, thereby restricting their access to the same.

Does it come with a free trial?

You don't quite know how the software is going to actually 'work' until you have tried it; getting access to a free trial might be just the thing you need to nail your decision!

Chapter 10: Step Ten - Promoting And Marketing Your Small Business

Of course, this final 'best' step is probably the one you've been waiting for all this while; that's why it is indeed kept to the very 'last'. It is well understood that to run any business successfully you really do need to have a solid marketing plan in place. That's what's going to give you that much needed 'edge' out there, after all, as far as taking your business to greater zeniths is concerned.

Let's get started, then, at uncovering just how we can effectively 'market' our business in order to meet those unparalleled levels of success that we have only dreamed of all this while.

Give it away for free!

Really? You might be thinking, how am I supposed to make any profit if I give my stuff away for free? Well of course you won't be doing it forever. Once you get those customers out there the opportunity to sample your product or service by offering it for free, they might just appreciate it to the extent that they convert to using yours over that which they have been accustomed to over time. In all probability you will get a lot more customers to try your product for the very first time if you happen to offer it 'free' to them, and that can dramatically increase the number of customers in that customer base of yours!

Be consistent in that e-mail campaign

You would want to ideally send an e-mail out to your valued customers once every week, wherein you provide something of 'value' to them. That is one of the best ways to remain connected with them and remind them of your presence, while at the same time showing them that you are dedicated to serving them with the highest standards of quality.

Try unusual marketing methods

If you choose to go the conventional route when advertising your product or services out there, you will find that you might end up spending a lot more money than you could afford. Often a most effective option is considering alternative advertising – for example, you could print an ad on a postcard and mail it to all the prospects in your area. You will be amazed at how many sales leads to your website you will generate in the process in a very short span of time and at virtually no cost.

Go in for joint promotions with other small business

You can offer to promote other small businesses out there to your customer database. In return, of course, you would expect those other small businesses to do the very same for you. This can be a great way to break into a market that would otherwise be largely untapped.

Create special deals for your existing customers

It is your existing customers that really give you the maximum business and not new customers out there; you want to ensure that you create special deals for them that will help them gain all the more confidence in your product or service and make them want to stick to using the same over time. It will make them feel special; now who on earth doesn't like to feel special every now and then?

You can even develop incentives for them that will ensure that they get rewarded with things like discounts every time they refer you to a friend of theirs.

Offer a premium version of your product or service

Once those existing customers discussed in the point above have decided to use your product or service, you might want to offer them a premium version of the same that they would be more than happy to lay their hands on, thus increasing your levels of profitability.

You could also introduce a 'package deal' whereby they could get an overall discount if they combined several products or services together. That would ensure that it would increase that 'transaction value' of theirs, meaning that you would make a lot more money in the process than you would were they to spend on a single product or service that you had to offer.

Conclusion

Over the course of this book we have seen just how the 'small' things in life can really be the 'biggest' by observing how we can leverage that small business idea of ours into fruition and maximize on our levels of profitability by ensuring that we reach those ambitious levels of success that all entrepreneurs dream of in the fledgling stages of business.

Thanks to the stellar tips provided in this book, you have seen that those dreams do not have to remain mere 'dreams', but can very well be converted to realities if you follow the basic principles that are firmly etched into this book.

The ten 'steps' that are outlined in this book are really most essential when it comes to working towards those entrepreneurial dreams of yours. If you follow them to the core we will find that it is really not all that difficult to make that business 'larger than life', even though in essence it might be 'small.'

Are you ready, then, to take charge of the dynamic process of working towards that small business dream of yours that has been harboring in your mind for ages?

Well, go on then, make it happen!

I will be more than happy to learn how this book has helped you in some way. If you feel you have learned something or you think it offered you some value, please take a moment to leave an honest review on Amazon. It would help many future readers who will be forever grateful to you. As I will!

To Your Success,

Adam Richards

Time Management

How To Get Your Life Back, Increase Productivity And Get More Work Done Stress Free

By Adam Richards

Introduction

What This Book Is About

In the first chapter, you will learn all about effective time management and we will discuss a few ways this skill can help you, regardless of what you do or who you are. In the next chapter you will learn how to set boundaries and how to say to no in situations that you might automatically said yes in the past, while in the same time being polite about it. Furthermore, you will find out 3 simple steps that you can take to begin saying no, in order to develop the skill of effective time management.

In the third chapter, we will go into the morning routine. We all have one, some are better than others though. That's why we will discuss the importance of a morning routine (also known as morning ritual) and how this single process can affect the quality of the rest of your day. You will also be given 5 ways that can make your morning ritual less hectic and more productive.

In the next chapter, we will discuss about prioritization, a fundamentally important factor of effective time management. You will learn 2 ways that you can choose from or use a combination of them, to better prioritize the tasks that require your attention. In the fifth chapter, you will learn about multitasking, what it actually is and whether or not this skill aids or hinders your time management endeavors. In addition, you will be given 5 tools that should you implement and follow will help you manage your time more effectively and will dramatically increase your productivity.

In the last chapter, you will learn how to eliminate distractions that eventually cut in on your time and stopping you from getting more work done. You will find out some guidelines that you can use to keep you focused and productive, while making sure you accomplish more in less time.

Once again, thank you for purchasing this book, I hope you enjoy it!

Chapter 1: What Everyone Ought To Know About Effective Time Management

As humans, we are hard wired to focus on things that need our urgent attention even when they are not necessarily important. This in turn makes us rush through our mornings struggling to catch our breath and even get furious when we get to work late.

When people hear about time management, they think about taking a hard-line stance on how they use their time.

One of the things that I have realized is that once you have a bad start to any day, there is 80% chance that the rest of your day will also suffer the same fate. If you are late to the office, chances are that you will require a few moments to compose yourself and catch your breath especially if you were almost running across the street to get to work lest you get late. This only gets worse as the day goes by. For instance, you may forget the morning meeting and even be forced to rush or riffle through your papers to get the documents that you need to present to the board.

Poor time management is something that a lot of us suffer from. As stated, we are hard-wired to take care of what we deem as urgent rather than what is important. Our daily schedules are full of activities that despite technological advancement, it always seems like there is never enough time in a day to complete them; this could be family, work or personal related. This makes it extremely hard for us to categorize which tasks are important and which ones are urgent making it extremely difficult to plan. Even if the plans that we make today are geared towards easing our burden in the future, we tend to be very busy all the time, but are never really productive.

Effective time management is a skill that each one of us regardless of where we work must develop and use in our daily life if we are to be productive. I can go on and on about how effective time management can positively affect your life but the truth is this, if you are comfortable with a less productive life, you shall never achieve all your dreams, goals and aspirations.

Time management is not rocket science; you do not need to spend long hours of studying to master how to manage your time effectively since it is a skill that you can develop easily and change the way your life works. This is not to say that there won't be times when we are extra busy.

For instance, times such as back to school, filing our taxes and completing important work projects are usually extra busy. Having effective time management skills will help you manage the time available to you as well as reduce the stress and frustrations that accompany these times. Below are just a few ways in which effective time management can help you regardless of what you do or who you are.

#1

Effective time management will help you work smarter rather than working harder. One of the most valuable resources available to you is time and once it is gone, you cannot get it back. Treating each task as a priority is a sure way to develop bad time management habit that eats into our time without adding our productivity. Making every task an emergency is very bad not only for our time but also for our well-being.

Effective time management helps you optimize your time by structuring your routine and mindset so that you are able to achieve more without much effort or stress. This works by identifying your daily routines and body energy needs at specific times and then delegating the most strenuous and important tasks to the times when you are at the peak of your productivity. Time management also goes a long way into helping you identify the "time waster" activities in your daily routine.

#2

Think of innovators like Steve Job. Although he may have had countless investor and shareholder meetings everyday he, had to set time apart to be innovative.

Effective time management is a skill that anyone who intends to achieve anything worthwhile must learn and practice. It is also important to note that effective management cannot be forced on you; it is a skill that will require a lot of self-determination and restructuring of personal life.

Since our daily life requires that we be flexible, learning this skill will go miles into helping you make wise and sound decisions in every circle of your life without being necessarily tied down to a restrictive routine. Developing good time management skills will help you determine the tasks that need to be accomplished in tandem with your life goals.

#3

Developing effective time management skills will also go a long way into helping you make snap decisions. How is this so? If you are invited to a cocktail party on a Friday night but you have prior plans with your family, you can be able to quickly determine which of the activities is more important to you; a few hours of happiness out with friends or the joy of spending time with family.

It shall also help you have a reason or explanation for those moments that you say no to tasks without feeling a lot of guilt. In the case of a manager delegating tasks to you, you can be able to explain to them that you have other tasks pending and thus the manager can be able to determine which task is of more importance.

#4

Effective time management also helps create order in your life. It is not just a skill that you can use in daily life but also one that can help you achieve your long term goals. The skill effectively creates a purpose in everything that you do by helping you to think about such issues like the reason why you have to do certain tasks at a certain time.

You are also assured of making positive strides to accomplish the small tasks that will build up to the goals you have in mind. Obviously, some tasks are easier to stand or do when they have a purpose.

For instance, cleaning is not something that most of us like but it is something that must be done if there is to be order and cleanliness in the home. This turns cleaning into a choice rather than a burden that we feel we must accomplish.

Being able to manage your time will help ensure that the areas of your life that mean the most to you are allocated the most productive time and this will contribute tremendously to the output of your whole life in general.

I have also found that being able to manage your time offers you more time that you can spend either with family or in pursuing something that you love. Effective time management is a skill that we all must learn in order to bring a sense of order and accomplishment in our life.

Chapter 2: How To Set Boundaries And Learn To Say No – (*Kind People Say No Too*)

As we have seen in the previous chapter, learning how to effectively manage your time will help you make snap decisions when you need to. Sometimes, a snap decision will require a no response. Humans tend to follow an unspoken social contract that dictates that when someone asks you to do something, your answer will usually be in the affirmative regardless of what other tasks you must focus on.

Learning to say no is an effective tool to cut out the less important activities in your life and focus on the activities that are most important to you. It is also very important that you be aware of how to differentiate between important and urgent tasks. Learning to set boundaries and saying no is very important if you are to succeed in your time management endeavors.

In the example in the previous chapter, we had looked at a decision that had to be made between going out for a cocktail party with friends and spending pre-planned time with family. Depending on what is more important to you (in this case family); one of these decisions will require a no. Setting boundaries on the other hand will help you know when you cross them and help you not to cross them.

When we say yes when what we want to say is no, we spend hours, days and sometimes months regretting the "yes" decision and feeling a lot of resentment while wondering why we said it. In most instances, saying no to a lot of us brings about feelings of shame and sometimes guilt. For example, when you say no to your children on a certain matter, you might feel guilty and as though you do not love them as much as they think you do or that you do not care. This is a perfectly natural response to 'no'.

Setting boundaries and learning to say no is about prioritizing and having the courage to love yourself and say no even at the risk of disappointing others. The most important thing is not to base your worthiness on the approval of other people. Instead, always remember that it is impossible to please everyone, even Princess Diana couldn't!

Learning to say no is symbiotic to productivity. Let us look at an example. If you were working on your computer on a strict deadline and you get a chat request from a friend whom you have not communicated with for long, what would your option be? Let the chat go un-responded to until you are through with your work or cut in on your deadline time and chat with your friend?

A lot of us will opt for the later and compromise on our work. This brings confusion and unnecessary adrenalin rush because we have to cover for the time we lost as the deadline approaches. Saying no looks like a mammoth task but it is not. We are all faced with different scenarios on a day-to-day basis. Learning to say no will help you filter out what is not important and give you enough time to deal with the important aspects of your life, which will greatly influence your level of productivity.

On the other hand, we cannot say no to everything. Developing an effective time management schedule and skill will help you prioritize and recognize the things or activities that require a no and those that require a yes. It will also help you create a strong will and inner strength. Even though saying no or setting boundaries is a bit of a task, there are some simple steps that you can take to ensure that you develop the skill of effective time management.

Step #1 - Create a mantra-

When you are sure you are going to say yes to someone you really want to say no to, it helps a lot to have a mantra. A mantra does not have to be a chant; it can be anything. A mantra is just something that you can use to remind yourself of your inner strength.

An effective skill is to have a ring, bracelet or necklace that you can stroke when the desire to say yes overwhelms you. Another effective tool is to have an actual mantra. In this case, choose something that adds more power to your resolve; "I can say no" is a good one. Tailor the mantra to your difficulty to say no.

If you have a lot of difficulty saying no, choose a strong mantra that helps you choose discomfort over resentment.

Step #2 - Keep a journal

One of the things that we have looked at is how after saying yes, we walk around being resentful especially when we fail to set boundaries. When you are feeling resentful, write this down and note all the times that you experience this. This can help you to recognize which situations make you feel the most resentment.

Step #3 - Practice

Saying no is something that develops over time but like everything else, you have to practice. There are individuals in our lives that we cannot be able to say no to instantaneously. It helps to start small. Start by saying no to small matters that concern only you and then move on to smaller matters that concern other people. A mantra to help you in this is, 'my plate is full' or 'sorry I cannot take that on right now'.

Setting boundaries will help you greatly in determining what is and what is not important and will also help you achieve more in the areas of your life that matter the most. Setting boundaries also requires that you set up a schedule that you can follow. A schedule should not be too restrictive and should afford you some flexibility.

Chapter 3: How To Create A Productive Morning Routine - Daily Planning 101

There are a thousand and one ways that each of us starts our morning. Although some of us start our morning much later, all of us have a specific time that we consider morning. Productivity is usually very high in the mornings hence it is important that you accomplish as much as possible during this time. This makes a morning routine a very fundamental part of effective time management as well as productivity.

There is no ideal morning routine because all of us have different things that we feel are important to accomplish in the morning. While my morning may be used to working out, someone else might use this time to accomplish some other task. Regardless of your morning ritual there are ways, tips and skills that you can use to ensure that your morning routine is productive and well managed.

Mornings are the perfect time to be creative, exercise as well as have some 'me time'. Additionally, science has indicated that a person's willpower is strongest in the morning. This means that if we want to be productive, we must take advantage of these and perform tasks that will be more difficult as the hours pass. How you spend your morning is also a precursor to how your day shall progress. In fact, a calm and productive morning will yield calmness and productivity throughout the day, while a hectic and frantic morning ritual will yield a lot of discord during the day.

In this chapter, we shall look at the ways you can make your morning less hectic and more productive while ensuring that this productivity carries on throughout the day.

#1 Plan

Planning is vital to every single thing that we do and your morning routine is no exception. At the end of your day, create a plan or a 'tomorrow's list'. On this list, write down all the things that you would like to complete in the morning. Ensure that you plan the hardest activities to be done first. This is called "eating a frog". Sounds yuck, right? This is just a hypothetical frog that symbolizes accomplishing the hard tasks earlier in the day; research has indicated that if you perform hard tasks that require a lot of willpower in the morning, the rest of the day will be easy for you. After creating the list, place it in a place where it shall be visible first thing in the morning making it easy to follow when morning comes.

Repeat this process every day to create order in your mornings. In order to avoid having too many tasks in the morning, choose your outfit before getting into bed and keep your keys and cell phone in a place where you don't have to rush around the room looking for them in the morning.

#2 Not all technological advancements are time management friendly

Technological advancements are superb but in the case of effective time management, they can be a hindrance. One of the most annoying things that each one of us has done on one occasion or the other is to hit the snooze button on our alarm clock. In effective time management and productivity, the snooze button is not your friend. It cuts in on time that you had preplanned for.

Contrary to what people think and believe, none of us is very fond of waking up (especially if you were having a nice dream) but we force ourselves to. Rather than using an alarm clock, I would suggest that you use a Jawbone, which gently vibrates on your wrist which is contrary to an alarm clock that jeers you awake.

#3 Make priorities easier

If your priority in the morning is jogging, place your workout clothes together in a place where they are easily reachable. If your morning priority is working on your project, ensure that all the materials related to the project are placed together.

#4 Exercise

Dedicate a minimum of 20 minutes of your morning ritual to exercise. Exercise in the morning has been proven to be very effective at boosting your mood as well as giving you a radiance and energy that will last you the whole day.

For me, going for a run does the magic. It invigorates me and works as a way to clear my mind and focus on the day ahead.

#5 Prepare for the day

Depending on what you do for a living, it is also important that you prepare for work. You need to take a shower, take breakfast and put on the right attires for your job. I have realized that this in itself improves on my mood and prepares my mind to start work.

You should already know that you should eat breakfast as a king since it gives your body energy to start the day on a high footing. Dressing smart on the other hand boosts your confidence, which helps you radiate positive energy.

#6 Grace period

If you have a pre-planned morning schedule that you created the day before, you will find that you can be able to manage your time better in the morning. This can afford you the luxury of never being late in getting to work or being late for any meeting. A very effective skill to cultivate is to always allow a grace period of 15 minutes before getting into a meeting. A 15-minute grace period is ideal since it helps you to arrive for the meeting with grace and dignity compared to the shame you would feel if you had to rush through the conference doors after being 15-20 minutes late.

#7 Review and be flexible

Review what needs to be done in the morning-Situations are bound to change overnight. You could have wanted to do something in the morning the day before; however, the situation might have changed overnight prompting you to do something different. Therefore, such things like checking your emails, social media and all instant messengers can help you know what needs to be done now based on the level of importance.

You can also respond to emails from clients, your work colleagues, your boss, your friends and anyone else who contacted you when you were away from work. Doing this also helps you to get rid of clutter by helping you to focus on what is important without feeling as if you are missing something important. Once you have responded to emails and instant messages, you don't get to think too much about issues that could distract you from doing what is important.

Creating a powerful and effective morning routine will ensure that you have the energy and correct mental attitude to tackle the rest of the day. Additionally, since a morning routine is geared towards helping you manage your morning time well, you will also be more productive during the day.

Early to bed, early to rise makes a man or woman healthy, prosperous and wise. Benjamin Franklin

Chapter 4: How To Master The Art Of Prioritization – (*There Is A Difference Between Important And Urgent*)

Prioritizing is also fundamentally important to effective time management. As we have seen, we tend to be more aware of what is urgent rather than what is important. Prioritizing does not mean that you give importance to tasks. It means giving credence and letting the activities that count come first and leaving the other tasks for later. There are different approaches that you can use to prioritize what is important and what is of lesser importance to you. There are two main ways that you can use to prioritize items on your to-do list

1-Tackling the difficult tasks first

In this approach, you tackle the hardest tasks first before moving on to the more mundane tasks. The reasoning behind this is the same as the example of "eating the frog" that we had looked at in an earlier chapter. Tackling the harder and biggest tasks first is ideally meant to ease the anxiety and pressure that might essentially hinder you from accomplishing anything.

For instance, let us take the example of a teacher. If the hardest task that they have for the day is grading the midterm papers, they might opt to do this before moving on to other tasks. In order to experiment with this method of prioritization, you need to be aware of what is harder to do for you and which tasks are relatively easy. This will require you to use your to-do list to determine what is harder.

2-Tackling easy tasks first

In approach number two, you first do the tasks that can be done in minutes and with minimal effort. One of the advantages of using this method is that once they are done, you have less inconsequential tasks distracting you from achieving or completing the harder tasks.

If we were to use an example, doing small tasks such as responding to emails, returning phone calls and doing some reading might all count as small tasks that you can do before moving on to other high yield tasks. This method is very effective at helping you finish easy to do small tasks that might build up to other bigger tasks.

Regardless of which method you use to prioritize, it

is important that you prioritize. There are those who believe that just one method is not enough to help you prioritize well. By combining these two methods, some people have been able to come up with an ideal way to ensure that they have their priorities in order.

You can also combine the two methods by starting making your to do list and then adding priority stars to each time. The items that have the highest priority should get a five star while those with the least priority should have a one star.

The important thing to remember when you are combining these two methods is that the tasks that fall on your to-do list do not have to be big tasks; your to-do list should reflect your work schedule. In most cases, you will find that small tasks barely make it to the list or warrant a star. Prioritizing is a very effective way to overcome procrastination.

An important consideration to have in mind when choosing which method to use is by understanding how you work. You will find out that some people are more comfortable with getting easily doable stuff out of the way before moving on to the harder stuff while others are more comfortable with handling difficult tasks first then moving on to easier tasks.

Prioritizing will also require that you be a bit flexible. There are days where I will get out of bed with my writing fires stoked and be writing by the time 7 a.m. comes and there are days when I feel that I have to go through every unread email in my inbox before I move on to something else.

It will also require that you be aware of the times that you are most active and productive. For me, to give you an example my peak hours fall between 8am-1pm after which I am less productive for a few hours. This effectively helps me prioritize on which tasks I should perform when I am very productive and which one I should do when I am less productive.

On most days, I usually push back reading my emails

into the late afternoon when I feel like I am forcing myself to write. I have found that this trick also helps me relax and get back energy to move on. To prioritize well, it is also important that you choose an ideal task management system.

The two most common task managers are the starred system and the scheduled task system. You can choose either one of these methods that you are sure will help you better. Personally, I prefer the starred system because it helps me have accompanying priority to each task and encourages self-discipline and trust.

Once you are able to prioritize, you will find it easier to work through a busy work schedule with minimal anxiety, panic and stress. The system of prioritization does not matter as long as you choose one that works well for you.

You should not fall victim to a set dogma until you have been able to try out each of the systems and have found which works well for you. If you already have a system that seems to work well for you, there is no need to change to the two systems that we have discussed.

As I have said, the systems do not matter. It is easy to give up or mess up an already working system in the hope that the other system will work only for it to be a complete failure.

Chapter 5:
Multitasking - Ally Or Enemy?

It is not unheard of to hear busy people proclaim how good they are at multitasking. Whether you are good at it or not is not the question.

The question is whether multitasking is a good tool for effective time management. The answer to this question is rather a two edged sword.

For some people, it is easier to perform two tasks at the same time while for others it is a bit difficult. What exactly is multitasking though?

Multitasking originated from the IT (information technology) industry. It is referred to as the parallel or interleaved implementation of two or more jobs. There are proponents of the skill that feel it is an essential life skill that helps one move fluidly between different tasks and work areas.

On the other hand, those who oppose this skill claim that it wastes a lot of time that could be used to complete one task before moving on to the other task. Personally, I am of the view that multitasking is counterproductive to effective time management.

Below are just a few of the cons that are associated with multitasking.

Multitasking Side Effects

#1 Less concentration

A study conducted by Stanford University found that people who were exposed to multiple streams of electronic information did not pay attention. This same principle applies in real life.

It is almost impossible to give two or more tasks your full attention without causing a conflict. Juggling tasks will create an urgency around you that never goes away.

#2 ADD and decrease of IQ

Multitasking has been linked with ADD (attention deficit disorder). Experts compared multitasking to playing tennis using two balls and found that constant jumps between tasks leads to reduced performance and productivity and gives someone the symptoms of ADD.

Additionally, a study conducted by Kings College in London found that constant exposure to email and other technology friendly multi tasks temporarily lowers the IQ by 10 points.

#3 Increased downtime

Multitasking has also been found to be increase downtime in workers. This is because when you leave a task and move on to another task, it is very hard to carry on the previous task from where you left off.

Due to streams of work competing for your attention when you are multitasking, it becomes extremely difficult to focus

There are also some benefits to focusing on one thing at a time:

Benefits Of Focusing On One Task

#1 More productivity

Focusing on completing one task prior to moving on to another means that you are able to give that task your complete and undivided attention. This is especially helpful in work projects that require perfectionism. Giving your attention to one task will also be translated into your productivity.

#2 Effective time management

Multitasking is a sure time waster. It is almost impossible and unheard of to perform two tasks at the same time in the same or little time than it would have taken you had you concentrated on one task then moved on to the next task.

Juggling between tasks is time consuming and counterproductive to your time management endeavors.

Now that we have effectively covered the cons to multitasking, it is only right that I give you some powerful tools that you can use to stop this and manage your time well.

Effective Time Management Tools

#1 Do one thing at a time

This is contrary to what multitasking is all about. When you find that you are inclined to multitask, stop, compose yourself and tackle one task at a time. You shall realize that you accomplish more and within a shorter time when you are not multitasking.

#2 Finish before you commence

Finish one task before moving on to the other. This will require some practice but once you get the hang of it, it shall be easier to practice.

#3 Prioritize

Prioritizing will ensure that small less important tasks do not take priority over bigger important ones.

#4 Close all notifications

Technology is very tempting; just when you are about to settle down into accomplishing a task, that is when the emails starts streaming in. Switch off your phone notifications and any notifications that might tempt you to multitask or make you deviate from your main task. Instant messengers are a complete NO if you are looking for an effective way to end mental clutter.

#5 Eliminate interruptions by using productivity apps

The truth is that interruptions are cleverly disguised multitasks. This could be email notifications or ringers and beeps. It is almost impossible to ignore an email if you get the notifications; it has something to do with how we are hardwired. You may want to use productivity apps like SelfControl to keep yourself focused on what is important.

Chapter 6: How To Eliminate Distractions And Get More Work Done In Less Time

Distractions come in many forms; some are good while some are loathsome. They are a hindrance to getting things done. Most times when you are working at your desk, you might get email notifications that distract you from what you are doing. Although this is not bad, there is a cause of concern when you start longing for the distraction so that you can stop your task. Eliminating distractions will help you accomplish more in little time. Below are guidelines that you can use to eliminate distractions and ensure that you accomplish more.

#1 Train your brain to focus

This is a fundamental part to eliminating distraction. Even though you might use headphones or other means to block out external stimuli, your brain is still the biggest distraction there is. If your brain is jumping from one topic to the other on unrelated subjects than what you are aiming to accomplish, there is no way you can remain focused. Training your mind can be done by learning how to control it.

In most instances, training the mind is just as simple as paying attention to your own attention and stopping impulses before they take root in the brain. Meditation is also another effective way to train your mind to concentrate on specific aspects at a given time.

#2 Break down huge tasks

It is easy to get distracted when the task seems too big and impossible. It might even cause you to procrastinate. Huge tasks become easier to accomplish when they are broken down into easier smaller ones that when combined ensure that the big task is complete. Research has also found that it is easier to get motivation to accomplish smaller tasks than it is to get motivation for larger tasks.

#3 Track your time expenditure

As indicated earlier, distractions come in many forms. To remove distractions in your daily routine, it is important that you track how your time is spent. This will assist you to learn which tasks attract a lot of self-distraction. A handy tool that you can use is a time tracker app that can be installed on your smartphone.

#4 Block all distracting websites and apps

One of the most common distractions is the web. When that email notification comes in and you are tempted to check what it is, the possibility is that you will also be tempted to make a brief stopover on FaceBook and make a few comments and before you know it, 30 minutes are gone.

There are applications and software that restrict specific website visits at specific times. So, use these to eliminate web distractions. Productivity apps can help you discover how productive you are within a certain period.

#5 Create a schedule

As we have seen throughout this book, a schedule is very essential in helping you manage time. It is also effective in limiting distractions. If you set a schedule, it indicates that you have every intention of following it and it is harder for you to get distracted.

Conclusion

Effective time management is a necessary life skill that will ensure more productivity in your life. It will also go a long way into helping you achieve your life goals as well as be in better control of your life and your time. If you implement all the skills that we have discussed, you will never have to rush at the last minute to get to your meeting or have a hectic unplanned morning. Your life will be seamless.

I will be more than happy to learn how this book has helped you in some way. If you feel you have learned something or you think it offered you some value, please take a moment to leave an honest review on Amazon. It would help many future readers who will be forever grateful to you. As I will!

To Your Success,
Adam Richards

DISCLAIMER AND/OR LEGAL NOTICES: Every effort has been made to accurately represent this book and it's potential. Results vary with every individual, and your results may or may not be different from those depicted. No promises, guarantees or warranties, whether stated or implied, have been made that you will produce any specific result from this book. Your efforts are individual and unique, and may vary from those shown. Your success depends on your efforts, background and motivation.

The material in this publication is provided for educational and informational purposes. Use of the programs, advice, and information contained in this book is at the sole choice and risk of the reader.

Negotiation

How To Nurture Your Negotiation Skills, Overcome Any Objections In Life And Get The Best Possible Deal Always

By Adam Richards

Introduction

What This Book Is About

In the first chapter, we will discuss the basics of negotiation and the importance of this skill. After all, we are already negotiating in several situations in our lives, so it would be wise to improve upon it and learn how to get around arguments.

In the next chapter, you will learn about this crucial

factor in all negotiations "Preparation". I cannot stress it enough. You will learn how to prepare, how to plan your strategy, how to set your goals and objectives and how to determine your last option.

In chapter 3, we will discuss 5 top-notch negotiating strategies that can be used in negotiations and furthermore, we will go into 10 ways that should you implement properly into your approach, will make you more persuasive and thus increase your chances of succeeding with your negotiations.

In the next chapter, you will learn 11 ways on how to become a more diplomatic negotiator, a crucial skill that can help you negotiate better and get what you want, anytime and anywhere. Furthermore, you will learn in detail about the types of questions that you can ask during negotiations and you will also be given 6 additional questions that you can ask while negotiating.

In chapter 5, you will learn about the 6 different categories of objections and then we will discuss the 6 most common objections that you can face while negotiating, and what they actually mean. Furthermore, you will learn how handle such objections using the 3Fs strategy, plus some additional objection handling tips.

In the last chapter, you will learn how to evaluate the outcome and close the deal successfully, unless of course you have not met your target objective. You will be given a few "desperate" actions or things that you can do at the time of closure and some strategic close phrases you can use to close your deals.

Once again, thank you for downloading this book, I hope you enjoy it!

Chapter 1: Negotiation 101: What It Is And Why It Is So Important

Going by the conventional definition of negotiation, it is the discussion that takes place between two parties to reach an understanding, resolve differences or gain advantage through coming up with a viable solution. In simpler terms, communicating in an interactive way is what negotiation is all about.

Negotiations can occur at different places; it can take place between close friends or family members, in corporate circles, political parties, or even between national and international leaders.

We all negotiate in various capacities and in different roles. Negotiation, in its varying forms and formats, keeps on taking place even when we may not realize it. As workers, we often negotiate with our co-workers and subordinates for getting work done; we often negotiate with our seniors or boss for some professional reason or for getting our leaves sanctioned.

We also negotiate at home; for instance, negotiating with your kids to do their chores or with your spouse to get things done. We also negotiate when we go shopping to get the best deals. Basically, we are always negotiating.

Negotiations are conducted either in order to edify something new or to resolve some existing conflict. There would be two or more parties who would be exchanging their ideas, suggestions in presence of conflicting goals that cannot be achieved independently.

Negotiations will include some or all of the following situations:

One party trying to make the other party to comply with certain demands

Modifying the opponent to compromise

Inventing a viable solution that would cater to all objectives

Why It Is Important To Negotiate

Now that you understand what negotiation is, let us discuss why it is so important to negotiate. Negotiation is important for several reasons. There are many situations and instances where things cannot be simply black and white; or where we cannot demand what we want blatantly.

In such situations, we ought to reach an agreement after negotiations.

During negotiations, you follow the primary objective of subduing conflicts that come in the way of decision-making. It is initiated only when it is sure that there is enough scope and span for mutual adjustment. Negotiations take place to bring in effectual and amiable agreements, achieve the desired objectives, build in positive interpersonal skills and consequently bring in more productivity on board.

There is a thin but clear demarcation between confrontation and negotiation. While confrontation is completely one-sided and accompanies arguments, negotiation takes place via discussions backed up with willful compromise. When negotiating, you do not brand yourself as right and the opponent as wrong. Instead, the focus is on logical persuasion. Negotiation is a vital skill that helps in building, maintaining and sustaining personal and professional relationships. It is not just about getting things done your way, rather how we equate

with others in our lives.

Normally, negotiations will be ruled out when there is no room for discussion and when the different parties involved are rigid enough to be influenced. In a nutshell, negotiations can only be conducted where there is a will for it to happen. As a negotiator, you need to be understanding and flexible enough to adjust your position and stance according to your opponents' situation. The process of negotiation involves exchange of ideas, information and plans. The proposals and suggestions gradually evolve during negotiations as you contemplate different options.

In order for negotiations to take place effectively, there has to be mutual flexibility and understanding. Both or all the parties must make ample proposals to break the jinx or lockout. During negotiations, if you feel that the other parties are not agreeable, there is a high likelihood that you will not concede defeat and thus you may end up at a crossroad and not moving forward.

Get Around Arguments

We all come across such situations when it is difficult to have things our way. People around or with us may not agree with our point of view and it becomes tough to make them concede to our stance. The best way to overcome disagreement is through negotiations where the parties involved can make amiable compromises.

Negotiations are a wonderful replacement of arguments whenever we want something with an aim to win the deal in a positive way. Negotiations neither offend anyone nor causes loss to either party as it is based on mutual benefits.

With negotiation being part of our daily life, it is important to become an effective negotiator to meet your goals in a subtle and agreeable way. You can learn this skill and can develop it further to help yourself in many ways. In the subsequent chapters, we will look at how you can become an effective negotiator.

Chapter 2:

Preparation Is KEY: Have You Done Your Research?

If you want to yield no fruits during negotiations, lack of preparation is the way to go. Preparation is indeed a key to fruitful negotiation as it helps the negotiator in capitalizing over his or her strengths and exploiting the other party's weaknesses.

Effective negotiation cannot be conducted randomly. Whatever the situation is, careful planning and preparation will help in being familiarized with the root cause of the conflicts and other party's stance in tackling it. Psychologically also, preparation will give you an edge over your opponent and confidence would prevail in the whole dealing.

Do not undermine your opponent as your lack of preparation would be clearly evident during the discussion and it would be used to your disadvantage. Consequently, your lack of planning will do more harm than good.

What And How To Prepare

So, you want to negotiate that big deal for your company or want to get your spouse or child to do something. How do you prepare? We will look at the different ways you can prepare for negotiations to ensure that you arrive at a suitable and favorable solution.

Plan Your Strategy

Prepare yourself to stay equipped with the right kind of strategy. Your inceptive offer or suggestion will set up the benchmark for the negotiations. Setting up a strategy would keep you on a confident pedestal and set the discussion on the right track.

The right kind of strategy would be the one where you can give something without affecting your position. Strategic moves will also impart your foresight and enable you to gauge the happenings.

Goals and Objectives

Nothing would work if the goals of the negotiations are not pre-determined. It would be almost like not knowing the destination and walking around aimlessly. Prepare your mind about the objective before beginning the negotiations.

The goals and objectives would act as a steering agent and would drive you right through negotiations. Furthermore, you will know exactly what you want and you will not accept anything less.

Options and Choices

Before you can even begin the negotiations, there is need to know what your options and choices are. I mean, although you may want to achieve a goal, what if the other party does not cave in. What is the next best alternative?

In fact, keep a backup of 2 to 3 options that would help close the negotiation on a qualifying note and save you from frustration. These backed up options can be referred to as 'BATNA' - Best Alternative to a Negotiated Agreement.

Hide or Reveal

Be prepared what information or facts have to be revealed or concealed during negotiation. This preparation becomes significant in case of corporate, political or business as there may be many dimensions to the discussion that would have interrelated connotations. Be prepared with your arsenal and be judicious in firing.

Furthermore, you have more power when you have important insight or information that the other party does not know since you can use this to your advantage.

Linking and Connecting

It is also critical that you not only know your opponent's goals but also link these goals with foresight. In fact, negotiating is all about connecting all the factors and options in a win-win way. Once the link is established, negotiation would meet the fruition. Moreover, this linkage can be possible only if there is smart preparation by the negotiator.

Fixate the bottom line

Conduct meticulous research to determine the last offer that would act as your final resort. Staying prepared this way will help you in being confident and you would be able to put your foot down, if required. Many times, negotiators have to unwillingly and disappointedly settle for a compromising deal.

Staying prepared with bottom line will act as a framework and let you play within the boundaries. However, this can act harmful as negotiation may be hindered due to rigidity of the set bottom line. The key would be to set a realistic yet resourceful boundary.

Chapter 3: Killer Negotiation Strategies: 10 Ways To Become Extremely Persuasive

None of us is born being the best negotiator. Negotiation is a skill that can be honed with the help of certain strategies. Although we negotiate innocuously in our day-to-day lives, we need to learn some important strategies so that we can take our negotiations skills to the next level and be the best negotiators.

These strategies would be equally effective in getting work done by your kids as well as in closing a coveted business deal. Basically, when you are an amazing negotiator, you are sure of receiving only the best deals. Let's get started with the strategies to use in shaping you to become the best negotiator.

#1 Creating a Lull

This is one of the most effective yet the most undermined and unutilized negotiating strategies. While negotiations are in the process, do not give in to haste and speed. Rather, take a slight pause so that a lull is created in the whole discussion. There may be several attractions and giveaways from the opponents' sides. Do not rush into them.

Taking a break will show your independent demeanor and allow you to negotiate freely and without any psychological baggage. Don't be too quick to give in to what your opponent is offering. Take your time to always evaluate your options to know if you can still get a better deal than what is being offered.

#2 Being Mr. /Ms. Know It All

Having adequate information before venturing into negotiation is a useful strategy. Do your homework well in advance or else you would be short of ideas and words while in discussion. In case your mind goes blank and you cannot think of anything to say to your negotiating opponent, just stay quiet and take a pause from the proceedings. This will serve dual benefits.

While you will get ample time to gather your wits and ideas, your opponents will take it as your silent signal for being unsatisfied. Who knows, this pause could be just what you need to strike that deal. Never show your opponent that you are not aware of certain information even if you don't know since they will use your weakness to emerge victorious in the negotiations.

#3 Put on Your Opponent's Shoes

This strategy works best many times, as it gives you a fair idea of what exactly is going on in the mind of your opponent. There are situations where many complicated and high-end strategies fail and the best way to get on track is to simply understand your opponent's point. This will help you even know their next step before they even put it forward during the negotiations.

#4 Exude Self-belief

One of the well-known killers of negotiations is desperation. However desperate you may be to clinch the deal or situation, do not let your opposition get to see that. In all possibilities exude great self-belief and even be confident enough to walk away during the discussions. Your self-belief will safeguard your fears from being sensed by opposing negotiators lest they would take advantage of them.

#5 Splitting the Difference

This classic and safe strategy encourages amiability right from the beginning. Many negotiators spilt the differences fairly so that both the parties can get equated benefits. Fair individuals who believe in setting an equitable deal or arrangement usually adopt this tactic. This strategy is akin to compromising and the opponent is treated akin to an associate and not a competitor. This is strategy is very helpful especially when you need to offer a solution and walking away is not an option.

10 Ways To Be Persuasive

Being a good negotiator may not necessarily mean that you are persuasive. Being persuasive is the #1 strategy to being the top negotiator who gets his or her way. Even if you use these strategies, you cannot be the top negotiator if you are not persuasive. In fact, without persuasion, negotiation will lose its steam and would be like an ordinary discussion where one would agree and the other one will disagree.

From being persuasive to believing in yourself and being able to persuade your opponent that what you are offering is the best deal possible, persuasion is necessary during negotiations. Persuasion takes place in our lives involuntarily most of the times. We are persuasive in varying degrees while playing our multiple roles of a professional, friend, spouse, and parent or as a shopper.

Here are 10 ways to be more persuasive

#1 Start on an Agreeable Note

If you want to sell your point of view, buy their version first. Starting on an agreeable note has always rendered positive results. This strategy works psychologically as you are likely to gain several points in the mind of opponents and they become receptive to what you have to say.

#2 Be purposeful

Being purposeful will give you a reason to be persuasive. While kids can be persuasive without any logical reason, and it suits them well, grownups often hold themselves back until they have some valid reason to persuade others. When you have a purpose, you will be more confident in your tone and demeanor.

#3 Be a Good Listener

You need to understand that persuasion is totally different from pushing. Thus, listening is an integral part of being a good persuader. Those who keep on ranting and just believe in drilling their words into others often get nowhere.

Be persuasive by being articulate in speaking as well as listening. The key to persuade effectively is to know others' version and taking their argument in your style.

#4 Create Bonds and Connections

Smart persuaders do not leave out emotions or feelings. They suavely establish relevant and appealing bonds and connections that consequently work in their favor. This ability places them in a likable league and they are heard with better attention and inclination. Persuade others patiently and with empathy giving no space to rashness or impatience. This way, it is going to be much easier indeed.

#5 Reinforce Credibility

To be persuasive in real and effective sense, do not beat around the bush laying stress over facts. It is to be understood that sometimes mere 'black-and-white' perceptions get ruled out and subjectivity has to be roped in to influence others. Make a point to highlight and reinforce the strong point and credibility of others simply because you want the same from others. Giving respect and credibility to others will make them more receptive to your point of view's consideration.

#6 Offer Agreement

Persuasion is not about winning by hook-or-crook like a war. Effectual persuaders underline the belief that they don't have to win every negotiation. Rather, they are intelligent enough to backtrack when the situation demands. They think creatively and sometimes offer agreement by meeting the solution mid-way. It is all about giving in when you have scope and holding on when it matters.

#7 Know when to Keep Quiet

Strategic persuaders hardly beat around the bush with their verbosity. They know when to shut their mouth so that their presented arguments can work on the minds of others. After driving in your final point, just relax your vocal chords and let it work for you. One of the classic lessons stated by J. Douglas Edwards was:

Whenever you ask a closing question, shut up. The first person, who speaks, loses.

#8 Talk Swift to Corner Skeptics

If your opponents are known skeptics, be a swift and smooth talker. This would hamper their thought process and they would find in tough to pick loopholes in your point of view. Your rapid talk will have to be associated with expertise, intensity and confidence.

#9 Limit the Choices

According to our conventional thinking, 'choices leverage the chances'. However, this becomes paradoxical in case of persuasion. The more options or choice would be offered, the chances of persuading go down.

#10 Repeated Drilling

Though kids resort to such kind of persuasion technique, planned and tactical drilling can have some desired effect.

Repetition plays with human minds and it starts contemplating the concept, sometimes even subconsciously.

After discussing all these persuasion tricks, it is important to convey that these should not be applied blatantly or desperately. They would work best when applied proficiently. Overdoing these would render bleak results, as no one is dumb enough to not get the negative feelers. Your need to persuade your opponent itself proves they are not witless to know what is already known.

Chapter 4:
How To Negotiate Anything, Anytime, Anywhere

Getting What You Want: Anytime And Anywhere

Negotiating is not always about tweaking people's opinion and selling them your point of view. It is also about saving your hard-earned money while shopping and getting some worthwhile deals. Tactful negotiations often make things easier and affordable as they become available on your terms. Let's move forward to learn how to become a diplomatic negotiator so that you can negotiate anything you want:

#1 Be Imaginative

When you eye an object and want to negotiate its price, start thinking creatively. Just asking the seller to cut down the price won't be that effective. Offer him/her something so that he/she lets go something. If you are negotiating the price of a refrigerator, offer to buy your future washing machine from the same vendor. This would act as incentive and you don't have to negotiate much to get the rate cut.

When it comes to services like catering or laundering, you can for instance, promise the seller the chance of word of mouth publicity, which would give an impetus to their business. Trust me; they will happily negotiate the rates.

#2 Be Pretentious

Very often, we may have to act pretentious or phony while negotiating. What may be important to us must not be made obvious. Be discreet about something that you really want.

Don't let your desperation be obvious for that thing. Hang on to something frivolous that you would easily let go off.

#3 Gauge the Timing

Know the timing of certain things before negotiating, as this is going to be of great help. For example, when you want to clinch some discount on insurance premium, know the time when that agent would have to meet the targets.

Discuss and negotiate with that agent just before the deadline closes. He would be a little excited (read desperate) and likely to give away some discounts at that strategic time. Most of the bakeries and food stores tend to negotiate rates of their fresh delicacies just before their outlets are about to close.

#4 Be Understanding

In order to be an all time negotiator, you do not need to be vicious all the time. Things can be negotiated by being compassionate and understanding too. A chord or rapport needs to be struck with the other person so that grounds can be setup for conducting the negotiations. Furthermore, mirroring their emotions will catapult them into your court, making them easily negotiable.

#5 Tame your emotions

As discussed earlier on, there is a very thin line between an argument and negotiation, and emotions demarcate these delicately. As a negotiator, you need to learn how to control your emotions or else, a respectable negotiation can crumble into a verbal volley causing ugly fiasco. When emotions step into negotiations, the discussion is steered towards personalities and turns ego-centric.

#6 Take the Bitter Truth

One evident and bitter truth about the game of negotiation is that both the sides know that they are playing one another.

There would be some mixed degrees of acting and lying, invariably evident by both the parties. There are many instances where you identify the game of the opponent and maneuver your own cards accordingly.

In this situation, we must not consider the other person to be malicious, as we ourselves must be playing somewhat a similar game. This is indeed a bitter truth and helps in understanding negotiations.

#7 Turn the Tables

How many times has it happened that a salesperson has handed over their card to you at the end of a negotiation session and said, 'Call me if you change your mind?' If such a thing happens, turn the tables instantly by giving your card to the salesperson stating something similar. May be you sounded on the lower pedestal of negotiations initially but they may feel like giving a deal on your price later at the end of the month. Your confidence will be remembered by the salesperson and they may revisit the negotiation on your terms.

#8 Don't be Apologetic for Negotiating

Some of us are very defensive towards negotiating. This can be killing for effective negotiations. Always start with assertive stance. There is nothing wrong in negotiating while shopping, as stores tend to offer discounts whenever they want. So, why not negotiate for price cut when shoppers want. Starting assertively will launch you on a higher pedestal.

#9 Negotiate with the Right Person

It would be futile to negotiate with the person who may not be having authority to give you the best deal. So, contact the person who holds the authority and save your skills on people who cannot make it happen.

#10 Play Your Loyalty Card

If you are visiting some store again, don't forget to play the loyalty card to make negotiations easy. Loyalty never fails to work as all businesses want to maintain their set of customers.

#11 Broaden the Play area

While in negotiating talks, we at times tend to be focused on one particular aspect and ignore other plausible options. Broadening the options would click things faster and there would be something for everyone in the negotiations. Benefits are sometimes not in simple black and white shades. They can be in some different and better format. For instance, if you child goes to school with your opponents child, you can use that to your advantage and who knows!

Using Skillful Questioning in Negotiations

Questioning is yet again another strategy that would help in tilting negotiations towards your side. Do not start volleying the questions anytime or every time during discussion. Ask only when you want to gather some information. Questions can be asked when you want to check the information and knowledge level of your counterpart.

Questions can again be asked to gauge the negotiating ability and to know the behavioral pattern of your opponent. If the opponent is not very participative in the discussion and this is acting as a deterrent for negotiations, use questions to pull the other person out of the shell.

Questions can also be wonderfully asked for bringing the discussion back on track and meeting the goals appropriately. If the negotiations are becoming tense, use questioning to diffuse the tension. This would make everyone relaxed and comfortable.

Types Of Questions To Be Asked During Negotiations

The questions you may ask can be of two natures:

Restrictive Questions

These are short and precise questions that can be answered in monosyllables.

Expansive Questions

These questions demand elaborate answering and are asked for knowing about your opponent's demands, objectives, and behavioral pattern.

Learn the Art of Questioning

The type of questions asked during negotiations is as important as the timing. Consider the 13 below listed tips to know when and what to ask and win the negotiations in your favor:

Tip No1

Ask questions with a concrete plan in your mind. The question should not be vague and not throw the negotiating proceedings off track.

Tip No2

The questions should be targeted and not offending in any way. This would better your chances to win the negotiations.

Tip No3

The flow of your questions should streamline from broad to narrow. While the initial questions can be generic, later questions can be specific and targeted. For example, while negotiating rates for a second hand vehicle, first ask if maintenance records of the car are available. Later the details of type of maintenance can be enquired.

Tip No4

Asking a question at the right time makes a huge difference. Wrong timing can spoil everything and sometimes the loss can be irreparable. Also, ask politely. This would render a good example and put you in a better light.

Tip No5

Frame your question tactfully to get the right kind of information. The objective should be to extract useful response.

Tip No6

Ask open-ended questions starting with how and why. The opponent will have no other option but to answer.

Tip No7

Ask participative questions that would encourage negotiators to be part of the discussion naturally and wholeheartedly.

Tip No8

Be enterprising in asking leading questions so that you can drive your point in a guided manner. Use phrases like - I've pointed out, I suggest, Don't you think, Will you etc.

Tip No9

Some questions can be gentle for eliciting soft emotional responses.

Tip No10

A series of questions can be volleyed to build up the tempo of rapid discussion.

Tip No11

Some questions can be laced with flattery to strategically compliment the opponent negotiator.

Tip No12

If you are being aggressive in questioning, choose the correct time. One such aggressive question phrase is - 'Do you expect me to believe…'

Tip No13

Some questions can be really tricky, almost at the verge of being threatening such as 'Are you going to…or…'

Learn to transform your opponents' objections and concerns into questions. This would serve the dual purpose of refocusing on value proposal and get the opponents thinking your way.

6 Questions You Should Be Asking

#1 How did you arrive at your asking price?

#2 Is this offer negotiable?

#3 When would you like an answer?

#4 Will you get the offer in writing?

#5 Do you expect me to believe that this is the best offer?

#6 Don't you think my deal is better?

Chapter 5: The 6 Most Common Objections And How You Can Overcome Them

Negotiations will always be inundated with objections. They are perfectly normal to occur and call for legitimate presence.

Encountering objections and handling them should come with strategy as the gist of negotiations remain in this ability only. Once the real fears and apprehensions behind the objections are decoded, their handling will become easier.

If we talk about classifying objections broadly, there would be 6 categories. They are:

1. Direct Objection
2. Indirect Objection
3. Confusion
4. Service and Price objection
5. Practical Objection
6. Psychological Objection

6 Classic Objections

We will look at 6 of the most common objections and how you can deal with them in order to emerge a winner in negotiations.

Objection 1 - I am not sure so I want to think about it.

This conveys that the other person does not have enough time. Give them some legitimate time and follow up later.

Objection 2 – I have not seen this service/product so cannot try it.

This indicates that the value of the service/product hasn't reached them properly.

Objection 3 - I've always used another brand.

This means the person should be given more reasons and valid points to make a switchover.

Objection 4 - The other quality/brand has better warranty.

Endorse yourself even better.

Objection 5 - I can get the same thing elsewhere at a much lesser cost.

Sell your benefits in a better style. Give references

of others who would vouch for you.

Objection 6 - I'm not ready to do/buy this at the moment.

This indicates that they are confused. They do want to clinch the deal but are unable to rationalize. It is suggested to give them more information.

How To Handle Objections

One tried and tested tactic to handle objections is the 3Fs strategy. It refers to:

Feel

Feeling what the other person is objecting to and saying "I feel that…'.

Felt

Using the phrase: "Many of my (customers, known, associates, friends) have felt…"

Found

Stating: "What my (customers, associates, known, friends) have found is…"

This strategy will suddenly ease the objection that the other party has and makes them open up to listen to what you have to offer. They will also get the idea that their objections have been felt earlier by others also, making them eager to listen how they were resolved.

9 More Objection Handling Tips:

Tip No1

Do not stifle the objections because of two reasons: They would encourage you to come out with better solutions The other person will open up for further dialogue.

Tip No2

However vicious objections may sound, keep a positive attitude.

Tip No3

Let buyers/counterparts know you are on their side

Tip No4

Give multiple solutions so that the other person can choose better.

Tip No5

Don't stall your negotiation until the deal is really closed.

Tip No6

Use tactical phrases like – I have another option/solution for you; This is the right time to…., Let's be fair with….etc.

Tip No7

Acknowledge the objections and promise to get back to the issue

Tip No8

Do not postpone or ignore the objection or it may put off your prospect

Tip No9

Use balmy phrases like - I think I have not made myself clear...; you have brought out a good point etc, to diffuse the negative impact of objections.

Chapter 6: Evaluating The Outcome And Closing The Deal - And When Not To

Once all effort has been infused into negotiations, it becomes imperative to know and evaluate what has been the outcome.

As mentioned in the beginning of this book, it is important to determine the goal and objective of the negotiations, quite early before you start the negotiations. Now, bring back the same goals back into the picture and assess if they have been met or not. Your success in negotiating will be directly related to what you wanted and what you have attained.

Also, contrast the situation. See what it was then versus now. The difference would be the leverage of your negotiations.

Closing The Negotiations…Finally

If you want to close the negotiations, don't be abrupt. Irrespective of the results of your negotiations, closure should come in a proper and respectable way. Closing doesn't and won't always mean that negotiations have been successful. They may even be doomed.

There can be situations where closure would not be suggested for the presence of some hope of discussion between the negotiating parties. Closure should be decided mutually only when a thorough study of the situation has been conducted mutually.

Closure can be contemplated in case of:

Difference of ideas and opinion has been diminished

One of the sides relenting

Both sides needing time to reconsider and reflect over their options

During closure of negotiations, there may be chances of hostility on either side. However, do not lose your cool, or be excited over any of the matter. Sometimes, closure time is used in a tactical way to resolve or leverage the issues.

Usually, one of the sides remains under pressure during the time of closing. That side is usually the one that has put in lot of time and effort and has been anticipating some concrete results.

Some desperate things/actions done at the time of closure could be:

Storming out of the room

Offering last option

Stating to take it or leave it

Issuing final ultimatum

Change in tone or body language

Introducing new and fresh options

Acting indifferent etc.

Strategic Closing Phrases

The kind of strategic phrases that can be used in closing are:

Perhaps we can find some common ground

I am ready to let few issues go provided you do the same

Let us leave this matter for now

I'm willing/unwilling to work this way

I think we both disagree/agree here at this point

I'm satisfied/unhappy with this stance

I think we should finalize this

I'd like to think over this for sometime

Would you be willing to close the deal on this note?

Let's meet again later

We'll have to settle this some other time

Ideally, closing of negotiations should not be about who won, lost or scored more points in debating. It should rather be conducted in a diplomatic way to initiate respectable proceedings. Closing should be handled wisely to gain validation instead of forcing attitudes or opinions over one another.

Actually, each negotiation calls for unique and subjective closure. However, it should be conducted in a respectful way based on mutual understanding.

Conclusion

Like everything else (that matters), becoming a master negotiator will not happen overnight, it will take some time and will indeed require constant practice on your part. However, if you stick with the advice you have learned so far and you start implementing even bits and pieces from now on, you will surely become a great negotiator.

I will be more than happy to learn how this book has helped you in some way. If you feel you have learned something or you think it offered you some value, please take a moment to leave an honest review on Amazon. It would help many future readers who will be forever grateful to you. As I will!

To Your Success,
Adam Richards

DISCLAIMER AND/OR LEGAL NOTICES: Every effort has been made to accurately represent this book and it's potential. Results vary with every individual, and your results may or may not be different from those depicted. No promises, guarantees or warranties, whether stated or implied, have been made that you will produce any specific result from this book. Your efforts are individual and unique, and may vary from those shown. Your success depends on your efforts, background and motivation.

The material in this publication is provided for educational and informational purposes. Use of the programs, advice, and information contained in this book is at the sole choice and risk of the reader.

Made in the USA
San Bernardino, CA
11 July 2017